T0208431

TREES...

...God's HINT to Humanity?

Annette Palmer

"Annette Palmer shares with her readers the insight and godly perspective that she has experienced about trees. She reminds us of the importance of taking the time to better appreciate what God has given to help point us back to Him! She brings to our mind that trees are not only living symbols of God's saving grace but they are a beautiful evidence of God's creativity. They provide yet another means of bringing us closer to Him by pointing us heavenward toward Himself; Romans 1:20."

- Dr. Joe Ferrini, National speaker with Family Life; Author: "Love All-Ways: Embracing Marriage Together on the Special Needs Journey"; "Unexpected Journey: When Special Needs Change Our Course." (www.JoeFerrini.com).

"Annette's enthusiasm spills onto every page as she shares God's power, love, and care for details in our lives. You'll feel like you're snuggled on her couch with a cup of tea as she unfolds the way God seemingly uses something so familiar as trees to point us to Him."

- Nancy Beach, Author, Speaker, Blogger

"In a time when we all can use a little hope, Annette offers her unique perspective that's both moving and thought-provoking. You'll feel her passion as she takes you on her enlightened journey to connect with God and his unending love. A journey seen through nature and even more so, through trees. You'll no longer look at trees as just... trees, but instead, a heavenly footprint of God. A beautiful reminder that He is everywhere and a part of everything. I strongly recommend this book. It has opened my eyes and my heart."

- Terry Begue, Speaker, Author of Attract & Keep Customers for Life

TREES...
...God's HINT to Humanity?

Annette Palmer

WESTBOW
PRESS®
A DIVISION OF THOMAS NELSON
& ZONDERVAN

WestBow Press books may be ordered through booksellers or by contacting:

WestBow Press
A Division of Thomas Nelson & Zondervan
1663 Liberty Drive
Bloomington, IN 47403
www.westbowpress.com
844-714-3454

Because of the dynamic nature of the Internet, any web addresses or links contained in this book may have changed since publication and may no longer be valid. The views expressed in this work are solely those of the author and do not necessarily reflect the views of the publisher, and the publisher hereby disclaims any responsibility for them.

Any people depicted in stock imagery provided by Getty Images are models, and such images are being used for illustrative purposes only. Certain stock imagery © Getty Images.

Unless marked otherwise, all Scripture quotations are taken from The Holy Bible, New International Version®, NIV® Copyright © 1973, 1978, 1984, 2011 by Biblica, Inc.® Used by permission. All rights reserved worldwide.

Scripture quotations marked NLT are taken from the Holy Bible, New Living Translation, Copyright © 1996, 2004, 2015 by Tyndale House Foundation. Used by permission of Tyndale House Publishers, Inc., Carol Stream, Illinois 60188. All rights reserved.

www.TreesGodsHintBook.com

ISBN: 978-1-6642-1757-7 (sc)
ISBN: 978-1-6642-1758-4 (hc)
ISBN: 978-1-6642-1756-0 (e)

Library of Congress Control Number: 2020925481

Print information available on the last page.

WestBow Press rev. date: 02/26/2021

This book is dedicated to my friend and love, Bob.
Thank you for saying "I do" on our wedding day and
becoming a part of my own growth in so many ways.

I am so happy to share this moment with you.
Your love and support will never be forgotten.

"You will seek Me, and find Me."
Jeremiah 29:13

CONTENTS

FOREWORD

"God has made it plain to them. For since the creation
of the world, God's invisible qualities, His eternal
power and divine nature, have been clearly seen,
being understood from what has been made,
so that men are without excuse."
Romans 1:19-20

When someone says they hear from or have heard from God, it's not necessarily that they heard His voice. God speaks to each of us in ways He knows will get our attention. It might be through circumstances, through the Bible, or even through His creation. He is ever so creative to draw us to Himself.

I've had the blessing of getting to travel a good bit, and no matter where I go, seeing God's creation causes me to be in awe of Him. Seeing something like the expanse of the Grand Canyon gives one a sense of the vastness of God. Looking into a calm glass-like lake, seeing the mirrored image of the sky is another message from Him showing the awesome expanse of forever above us. We might even see images of God in the tiniest of creatures as we wonder how their little bodies can house a heart, brain, and other functioning parts. In living things, if we are looking and considering - we will likely find Him.

Annette has heard from God in nature. Her story and experiences have deepened her walk, directed her steps, and given her a story to share with us that draws us to looking up and directing us to God through nature and more specifically in trees. Her insights will open your eyes and heart to seeing things differently and perhaps more clearly about the ways of God and His plans.

As Annette shares with you in her writings, consider what God might be teaching you through nature. God points us to Himself in many ways. Consider the way God pointed Annette to seeing Him more clearly and how you might, also. Look around, look next to you, and don't forget to look up!

Cindi Ferrini
Author, National Speaker, Blogger, Radio Personality, Friend.

PREFACE

Over the years, I've had the privilege to serve God in my weekly group, the Titus 2 Women's Bible Study. The purpose of this group is manifold, but first and foremost, we come there to *grow*.

We come to *grow* as sound-minded women.

We come to *grow* as the church and for the church.

We come to *grow* and be all that we can be according to God's design for humans.

But most importantly, we come to *grow* and learn so that we can guide others to do the same.

Peter, in the bible speaks to us directly as we *grow*, indicating that our growth is through His Son, Jesus Christ. He is everything and all that we need.

> "His divine power has given us everything we need
> for a godly life through our knowledge of Him
> who called us by his own glory and goodness."
>
> II Peter 1:3

In a world where relationships, especially marriages, are increasingly challenging, my weekly bible study is a group specifically designed for women's unique family issues. Spiritual *growth* occurs weekly in our discussions. For the past two decades, my whole ministry has been based on it.

However, I'm writing this book to share a completely different *growth*. It's one that leads to an awesome connection - a connection with God through, believe it or not, TREES.

I had a stunning serendipity one season that led to a richer form of knowing God. It occurred when I discovered that He was most likely speaking through what He has made - what was all around us - nature.

After reading this book, I hope that you will connect with God in a newer and richer way every time you simply look outside.

Though you will read about other revelations from God through the world outside, this book largely centers on the biggest and grandest view of nature: TREES. This might sound wonky, but bear with me. By the time you're finished reading, you may come to realize, recognize and appreciate what I did: That on Earth, God is blatantly revealing Himself in the loudest way, through one of His largest and most awestriking creations.

<u>Ready for your first WOW?</u>

Three trillion. That's the staggering number of trees on Earth, according to a new tally that astounds even the scientists who compiled it.

Three trillion is a 3 followed by 12 zeroes, which is more than the number of stars in the Milky Way and more than the number of cells in a human brain. If the new sum is accurate – and other scientists think it is – the planet boasts roughly 420 trees for every living person.

USA Today, Sept. 2, 2015

Here's your second WOW:

Trees are mentioned *more than anything else* in the bible besides God or people. They are mentioned on the first page of Genesis, in the first Psalm, in the first book of the New Testament, and on the last page of Revelation. There is a tree associated with every major event in the Bible like the fall, the flood, the overthrow of Pharaoh, just to name a few.

Now, a third WOW: *(but not the last, there's more to come!)*

Every major *character* in the Bible is associated with a tree. Here are some examples:

- Noah received the olive branch (Genesis 8:11)
- Abraham sat under the oaks of Mamre (Genesis 18:1)
- Joseph is a fruitful bough (Genesis 49:22)
- Moses stood in front of the burning bush (Exodus 3:2–5)
- Elijah sat under a broom tree where he received a message of comfort from an angel (I Kings 19:5-7)

- Christ is described like a small shoot from a plant or tree (Isaiah 53:2)
- Christ, as the Messiah, is described as a branch (Isaiah 11:1, Jeremiah 23:5, 33:15, Zechariah 3:8, 6:12)
- Daniel, interpreted Nebuchadnezzar's dream of a tree (Daniel 4:4-12)

The same pattern is in the New Testament:

- The blind man saw people as if they were trees walking (Mark 8:24)
- Zacchaeus climbed the sycamore tree (Luke 19:1-4)
- The disciples gathered on the Mount of Olives (Luke 22:39)
- Paul wrote that Christians are like branches grafted into Israel's tree trunk, with roots that help us stand fast and firm no matter what troubles come our way (Romans 11:17-18)

There are more, but enough WOWS! *(For now...)* How about instead, *a sweet sentiment* about God and trees?

Every year, a tree trunk grows an indication of how old it is - one ring for each year of its life. God must really love trees. Every year, he gives them a ring on their birthday ☺.

I believe trees are the biggest HINT from God to humanity, and a most powerful invitation to know Him.

"Now this is eternal life: that they know you, the only true God, and Jesus Christ, whom you have sent."

John 17:3

May this book connect you more intimately with the heavens than ever before. If it is truly a *brand new* connection, then I pray that you will bond for the first time with the Maker of the universe.

Have you looked up lately? His divine power is imbued in every leaf on every tree.

ACKNOWLEDGEMENTS

Bestselling author, John Eldredge, who inspired me to start looking for God's biggest HINTS in nature through his book, *Epic.*

Cindi Ferrini - Author, speaker, blogger, radio personality, friend. National Speaker for FamilyLife for 20 years. Thank you for the back cover shot and inspiring me to the serendipity of Chapters 7, 9 and 11. Also, for teaching me that accepting a gift is like returning a gift to the sender. I hope you feel that way for your contributions you made to this book. What gifts to me.

Megan Werner, past voice student and writer. Over coffee, you started my engines on this project. Thank you for your wonderful editing. Keep *growing* and searching for the true meaning of life.

CJ, for helping me believe I could be a good Mom and teacher of spiritual things.

Julie Katona - Dearest friend and sister-in-Christ who inspires me every year with something that changes me. You also inspired Chapter 5.

Shannon Savage for helping me launch. You modeled the courage to move forward.

My loving niece, Brenda Norris. My tech advisor and cherished younger woman. (Titus 2:3-5)

Anthony Taddeo - the past praise team drummer, who doubted my HINT theory just the right way at the right time (Chapter 13).

Joanne Frank and Vicki Zeilinger for helping me start and develop the Titus 2 Women's Bible Study where I first shared this theory to an audience.

Brunswick Reformed Church, who continues to feed me the Word of God.

Nancy Beach for your friendship while I was fine-tuning this.

Dave Toom for building my guts. Thanks for your belief in me and for cheering me on while I ministered at church.

Nine year old Frankie from Sunday School - you changed the world! You reminded me about the burning bush!

Ralph Smedley for creating Toastmasters International on March 24, 1905, and refining my path of public speaking.

Brian Hardin at DailyAudioBible.com - who speaks my daily devotionals directly from the Word.

Claudia Sarhage Stephens, from Campus Crusade for Christ - for cold-calling me at USC on Oct. 22, 1974 at 4:30pm. Jesus saved me that day because you walked over.

Jim and Louise, better known as Mom and Dad Palmer, who have supported and loved me like their own since I became a part of the family. Because of your example and longevity in marriage, we were honored to both surprise you and then join you on an Alaskan cruise for your 50th Anniversary. Our family had the time of our lives and the trip ultimately inspired this entire book.

CHAPTER 1

GROWTH: GOD'S EPIC DESIGN

"The righteous will flourish like a palm tree,
they will grow like a cedar of Lebanon;
planted in the house of the LORD,
they will flourish in the courts of our God.
They will still bear fruit in old age,
they will stay fresh and green..."
Psalm 92:12-14

Every year at Titus 2 Women's Bible study, there is a theme that plays a major role in our studies. Sweetly, the heavens might have inspired the theme in 2006. My trees theory, which you will learn about as you go, was perfectly timed inside our season that year, which I named "Growing in God's Garden".

"Growing" is an interesting word, when you think about it. After all, whatever is alive grows! This includes plants, people, and even all our lovely appendages, that is noses, ears, hair, feet, etc. Humans are also meant to grow in the most important way of all: spiritually. It's true. Just like anything that grows in nature, one of the purposes for our spiritual growth is to reproduce!

In the Gospel according to Mark, we read this:

> "Still other seed fell on good soil. It came up, grew and produced a crop, some multiplying thirty, some sixty, some a hundred times."
>
> Mark 4:8

It seems, then, that our spiritual growth is a vehicle for knowing and practicing God's truths and then reproducing them. Those who accept His word will indeed grow in it, and then in turn give hope from it to others in a world filled with chaos.

The world today especially needs hope! I am writing this in the unique and challenging year of 2020. Looking around, I see hope often disguised as temporary solutions. Money, fame, self-medication, and relationships become counterfeit. Instead, the hope Christians share is a trustworthy message. In a world filled with so many false solutions, believers have the solid, truthful gospel. How refreshing for us.

God designed growth! We often forget that anything that is alive grows. From our first breath to our dying moment, we are creatures in flux. But this flux does not *always* point in a positive direction. To illustrate this, think of an apple on a tree. The longer it stays on the tree, the longer it continues to ripen and stay edible. But what happens once it is picked off the tree? Does it stop growing? Yes, but in a different way. In time, mold will grow and then the apple gets mushy and gross.

These negative changes - decay, atrophy, and mold…can also be applied to a person in the same way. Decay of the *heart* can set in when there is no *spiritual* growth.

Another word for this decay is *sin*, and we see it often in the Bible. God hates it. It hurts everything and everyone. The consequences can last for years. Can you relate to this feeling?

Does your church grow or is it atrophying? Ephesians tells us that the church is a living entity, meaning it should be a body of souls engaged in spiritual growth.

Many churches around the world however, are shrinking because they are filled with *decaying* souls. Why is this happening? If the body of the church is not growing with each other, then the congregation is *not* producing - or *reproducing* -meaningful fruit. This human and moral decay can also spread like mold - the wrong kind of growth - just as one bad apple can spoil the whole bunch.

Moldy or rotten apples release a chemical called ethylene that causes other fruits and vegetables to rot faster. What a parallel this emission is for *hanging around with the wrong crowd.*

The same way decay is dangerous for us individually, so it is an impediment to the church. As Christ's body, it is our earthly task to be on a mission of sanctification for ourselves and others, to be the pure bride of Christ and - to be the hope for the world.

> "...and to present her as a radiant church, without stain or wrinkle or any other blemish, but holy and blameless."
>
> Ephesians 5:27

This book is about growth. So now, I want you to take a moment to ask yourself the following questions:

Am I personally growing or decaying?

Am I helping my church grow or decay?

CHAPTER 2

THE CRUISE THAT CHANGED IT ALL

*"And if we know that he
hears us—whatever we ask—we know
that we have what we asked of him."*
I John 5:15

It's rare for me to talk about anything other than personal growth and how God wants us to conduct ourselves in our relationships in our Titus 2 Women's Bible study. However, this idea that we can witness His boundless love shown to us through believe it or not - trees, has been burning in my heart for many years. I am excited to finally get my message out in this book. Here goes!

Trees? I know what you're thinking, but as I said earlier, bear with me. The idea is laughable, sure. But there's a lot of insight to take away from it.

It all started back in June 2006 - the year this idea first sprouted in my mind.

I was on a gorgeous Alaskan cruise with my husband, Bob. It was a lovely trip packed full of excitement, even during the planning phase. There was something about planning that vacation that just moved me emotionally. What can I say? God designed me to excite easily!

Actually, this cruise vacation wasn't just for Bob and I, it was for the entire family. We were celebrating my in-laws' fiftieth wedding anniversary. Because of the size of our group, we needed to book the cruise at least a year in advance. That meant I had a year of anticipation leading up to what would become a pivotal experience in my spiritual life. I loved counting down the months and days to our trip on my calendar. Sometimes life feels more fun when we have something to look forward to.

Slightly off topic: I am a walker. Since I live my life in the fast lane, my daily walks provide me with some much-needed spiritual quiet time. During my walks, I pray, I think, I plan, or I simply worship while I listen to music or the Word online using Brian Hardin's "Daily Audio Bible" (which I highly recommend!).

During my walks in the months leading up to the cruise, I started praying more and more about something specific: our upcoming trip! At the time, I was thanking God simply for the opportunity to go on this trip for the pleasure I knew I would experience. I knew this trip was a part of His plan for me, but I had no idea just how important it would become for my spiritual growth.

I'll admit that I wasn't exactly sure what this cruise had in store for me besides a fun-filled week of quality time with my husband and his family, but I thought, there must be another reason. I decided to trust in God's Word -

> "And we know that in all things God works for the good of those who love him, who have been called according to his purpose."
>
> Romans 8:28

The month before our trip, during my walks I started getting creative with my prayers. Instead of just thanking Him for the trip, I started asking God for a favor: "Lord, teach me something new during this upcoming Alaskan cruise - something new about Yourself that I don't know yet."

These prayers only added to my excitement and anticipation. I knew what Matthew 21:22 said: "If you believe, you will receive whatever you ask for in prayer." When God heard my prayers, I couldn't wait to see what He had in store for me, whether it was a subtle answer or an answer that came like a big bang. I would have even been excited if it came much later. It didn't matter. I knew He'd answer this specific prayer, and maybe even have some fun doing it.

Departure day finally came! The trip was a blast from the moment we stepped on the ship. Bob's family is big, boisterous, and full of love - think of a classic "fifties" TV family. When I first met Bob, his mom played bingo, they lived on Hocking Boulevard, had a dog named "Boots" and the mailman's name was "Mr. Higgins"! All of this seemed right out of my first-grade reader!

The Palmers banter and support each other endlessly. How could I not feel amazing surrounded by all that loving energy? *Carefree* is still one of the first words that pops into my head when I reminisce about this trip.

On board, there was a delicious smorgasbord of food from around the world. There was top-notch entertainment. There were workouts, educational talks, and most importantly, fun!

I took a real shine to the track on the twelfth deck, where I continued my daily walks. After my walks, I usually headed over to the workout room that overlooked the bow. From there, I could actually watch whales frolicking in the ocean! There are no words to describe the awesomeness of witnessing a humpback whale while running on a treadmill.

CHAPTER 3

SEEING THE FOREST FOR THE TREES

"...they may be ever seeing but never perceiving..."
Mark 4:12a

This is where my Alaskan cruise gets interesting.

Most ships make pit stops at different ports along the way so that passengers can get off and do some mainland sightseeing. Before the cruise, my husband, while looking at the ship's brochure, asked me, "Which excursion would you like to go on?" I read them all and BINGO! I knew immediately which one! I wanted to go on the tour of the salmon farm! It was an excursion that explored how salmon spawn. (I hear you laughing!) The best part was that we would get to eat the salmon afterward! For readers who know me personally, they're probably not surprised that I chose an excursion where food was involved.

Oh no - the Salmon Farm excursion was booked solid! It left us no choice but to go on the only other excursion available for that day - a five hour train ride to the Klondike. The what? Sounds boring! And by the way, I thought, what's a Klondike? I don't know about you, but the only Klondike I'm interested in is the ice cream bar covered in dark chocolate and toasted almonds. Naturally I was a bit dismayed when I learned there would be no ice cream involved.

I found out later that the Klondike was a famous gold mine. Bob and I still hesitated to de-board the ship for this train excursion. Though it was more economical for us because it was one of the less-expensive ones, it didn't sound at all inviting.

This train was the excursion my in-laws had chosen. Now don't get me wrong; I love my in-laws and I love spending time with them, but I'm more of a doer than a sitter. Sitting on a train for FIVE hours didn't exactly spark my enthusiasm.

But there we went. Over those long hours, there was not much to do, but stare out my window. Yikes.

We did see a black bear. That was cool. But still, miles and miles we traveled without seeing much of anything moving but the train itself!

Surprisingly, after a while I wasn't as bored as I expected. Little by little, I found myself curious and pensive. I was surprisingly delighted to see some of the most sublime foliage ever. (Go figure - foliage?) We were in virgin territory, touched only by God's creative mind. It was what the Earth must have looked like before man got to it: pure foliage in every direction, that's all.

With my head propped up against the train window I gazed upon this Alaskan beauty. I couldn't help but ask the Lord why He created all of this foliage before man started developing the land. After all, it wasn't like there were a lot of people up there to appreciate it. Why would God create these picturesque scenes for nobody?

I started to wonder if Bob or my in-laws were wondering the same thing. Did God have a lot of spare time on His hands? In the end, I decided that it was none of my business for now, but that it certainly must be for His greater glory.

Who really knows? All I knew is that what I was looking at was beauty incarnate.

Then I started studying the actual ground cover as we rippled past. Ground cover refers to the low-growing, fast-spreading plants that keep weeds at bay. Again, I began to ask God how these seemingly lowly plants glorified Him. How did they fit into His plan, and perhaps a bit more callously, why would He even care about these plants?

Next, I saw further down in the soil, droppings of past seasons - a ton of leaves and scraps from plants already grown and gone. I supposed that waste would become fertilizer for the new growth. It reminded me of when my Dad used to tell me to unload the grass clippings from the mower bag around the fruit trees in our back orchard. The droppings would act as compost for the soil, bringing more growth and nourishment every year to the trees. Wow, I thought, God is a *recycler*!

At point, the train's engineer, who doubled as a tour guide, gave descriptions that started to peak my interest even more. He explained how Alaska's winters were brutal and that the plants endure some nasty storms, full of ice, snow and piercing winds.

I was baffled by the fact that these delicate plants managed to weather these incredible storms - and with ease. Some of these plants were nothing but clumps of thin blades of grass that stood firmly upright, even in the harshest of conditions. Gravity was no match for these hardy little plants - but how?

In my mind, the song "Defying Gravity" from the latest hit musical that year, *Wicked*, kept playing. I am a voice teacher by trade and interestingly, during the finale of my recital I sang that song. This was right before the trip (coincidence?). The message energizes me: "I think I'll try defying gravity..." No matter what daily life brings, people like you and me can fight back against the gravitational forces that try to pull us down.

I was witnessing this message firsthand right on that train: these tiny, little upright plants defying gravity, even in Alaska's most bitter of storms.

All of this called to my mind memories of the spring, when dandelions, tulips, and blades of grass grow long and thin and spread their tiny roots. Those plants defied gravity throughout the brutal rains and storms too. God must be behind all of this, I thought.

Why is it that when I drop an earring, it tumbles to the floor, but a blade of grass with fragile roots stand erect, withstanding the worst Alaskan storm? Why don't these little tiny roots cause the plants to wilt, wither or fall in the face of terrible weather?

I could think of only one spiritual explanation. Have you ever grown a plant by a window in your home? Did you notice that the limbs and shoots grow toward the sunlight coming through the glass?

When God made the Earth, before man, I'm just sure it was all about plants and praise. I believe that He fashioned these plants so that they would grow upward to praise Him, despite most any circumstance. In fact, you can see this upward growth in all plants; they're *all* drawn deliberately to the light! The light grows them into their fullest expression.

Check out this verse from John 8:12. Jesus proclaimed, "I am the light of the world." Both plants *and* people need light to function.

Who knew that photosynthesis from light was really a divine process? God knew, that's who!

There are two Bible passages that speak on all plants' predilection for praising the Lord. In these passages God exclaims His intentions, this time, for the worship from His lovely foliage.

"...let the fields be jubilant, and everything in them. Then all the trees of the forest will sing for joy; they will sing before the Lord...."

Psalm 96:12-13a

Expounding on this even further:

"The mountains and hills will burst into song before you, and all the trees of the field will clap their hands."

Isaiah 55:12

This is very similar to how we worship at our own church services.

As you can see, it's biblical that all foliage praises our Lord also!

Here's another WOW: *(I told you there were more coming!)* This time it's about ROCKS. Here me out on this one!

Have you ever dug around in your garden and discovered a bunch of rocks that weren't there the year before? How did they get there?

Sometimes, it seems like even the rocks want to worship by lifting themselves toward the light to praise God, like plants do. Go figure! Even though they're much heavier than plants, they still manage to work themselves up *against gravity* and move toward the sun. God provided light not just for foliage, but for the whole Earth, including rocks!

> "...And let them be lights in the vault of the sky to give light on the earth." And it was so.
>
> Genesis 1:15

On the site called *"Laidback Gardner"* of April 9, 2019, Larry Hodgsons states the science of why rocks migrate upward:

> "In colder parts of the world, a curious phenomenon often takes place: stones and rocks—from pebbles to rocks larger than your head—seem to magically grow like mushrooms in fields and gardens. Every year, gardeners and farmers remove the ones that rose to the surface and the following year, new ones appear. In parts of the Northeastern United States, they're so common they're called New England potatoes and stone fences are built of them. Or huge piles of them can be found where a frustrated farmer moved the larger ones ... often over hundreds of years (yes, they just keep on coming over centuries!).
>
> Farmers traditionally move the rocks out of their fields and use them to build stone fences.
>
> These rocks re associated with glacial deposits: soils pushed to the spot thousands of years ago by

glaciers mixing sand, clay … and stones of all shapes and sizes. The soil is full of them, often to great depths, and they keep migrating upwards over time … but why?

In cold climates, rocks and stones tend to migrate upwards due to the effects of freezing and thawing. The science behind the phenomenon comes from the fact that rocks are better conductors of heat than soil. As a result, as winter sets in, the rocks take heat away from the warmer soil underneath. The soil beneath the rock, now colder, freezes before the soil above and, since it contains water and water expands as it freezes, the soil does too, pushing the rock upwards through the unfrozen soil above. In the spring, at snow melt, the space under the rock fills with soil, supporting it. And so it moves upwards, year after year, until it pops up in your garden."

Well, that might explain Luke 19:40, when Jesus fired back because the Pharisees were trying to keep His disciples quiet about the miracles they'd seen. "I tell you," He replied, "If they keep quiet, the stones will cry out." What He seems to be saying is that the stones will cry out in praise of the Lord, no matter how long it takes them to inch their way to the surface to do it.

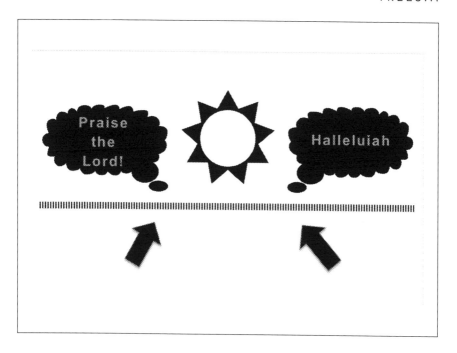

Plants and rocks. Before any man or animal walked on Earth, it was just plants and rocks–and they were all all stretching to bask in God's glory by growing upward - defying gravity. It seems that the will of all of creation is to reach God.

So then I started to wonder how plants keep their stamina up for so long; most humans can barely make it through a one-hour yoga class! How can plants constantly reach upward and defy these natural gravitational forces without exhausting themselves?

Well, you need food to live, right? So do plants.

In fact, the only way plants can maintain this constant movement is through constant nourishment. The Psalmist says:

"He covers the sky with clouds; he supplies the
earth with rain and makes grass grow on the
hills."

Psalms 147:8

So rain isn't just for nourishing plants, it's also a thoughtful
strategy God designed for plants so they can continue to praise
Him - unceasingly.

As you've read, rain water freezes and thaws moving the
rocks upward so *they* can also praise Him unceasingly.

The roots of plants meet the rain and feed off the nutrients
from the ground. Oh how they model our own praise! Rooted
in Him, and being nourished by His ever so grounded Word.
We also continue to grow upward to Christ so that we can defy
the gravitational force of the enemy.

"The thief comes only to steal and kill and destroy;
I have come that they may have life, and have it
to the full."

John 10:10

The foliage and ground cover in Alaska were valiantly
fighting natural enemies. Even with all the rough weather,
they continued to grow upward and endure all that came
their way.

It was an incredible epiphany that I knew we could all
apply to our own human lives as well. Like the plants grow

through water and nutrients, God offers the water of baptism and then His word becomes the fertilizer of our souls.

Are plants and rocks an example of how *we* should be using His water, nutrients and light to continue reaching for and praising our Creator?

CHAPTER 4

GOD'S LOVE SEEN THROUGH TREES

*"How great is the love the Father has lavished on
us, that we should be called children of God."*
I John 3:1a

So, I thought, with my head still leaning on the train window, if ground cover praises God, how do trees do it? After all, the Lord must have a special place in His heart for his oldest and biggest creations. Trees have the largest branches of any plant.

Suddenly my eyes focused on the most stunning feature I'd seen on trees. For the first time in my life I realized that all of their branches were rising upward. They seemed to be lifted towards the heavens in high praise. (What a WOW moment for me!)

One of the Psalms says this,

> "...all of the trees of the forest will sing for joy."
>
> Psalms 96:12

Did you ever attend a music concert that was loud and boisterous? Notice the fans in the front rows. It seems like an instinctual act to raise their hands toward the performer on stage because they are so "rocked" by their talent.

In the same way as concert fans, trees also reach their limbs upwards in praise. They are also the ones standing the closest to the stage, a stage brightly lit from the heavens. They love to focus on and worship their Creator!

And then it happened, my *eureka* moment. I sat straight up in my train seat like a bee just stung me. The shock wasn't from a bee; it was from a startling new connection to Christ that I made for the very first time. It was all simply from passing by thousands of trees. I realized:

BY USING A TREE, GOD MADE HIS BIGGEST PROVISION FOR HUMANITY!

I was dumbfounded. My mind started to erupt like a volcano. Jesus' greatest act for humanity was on a cross made from a *tree!*

Think about it! They're the largest living creature. And - they're everywhere.

Did God really place trillions of trees all around us as a *hint* to humanity?

This breakthrough only grew deeper in my heart and soul as we continued to whiz past what seemed like millions of trees. Trees, along with the rocks and other smaller plants, were *all* reaching upwards to praise God, modeling worship and reminding us of salvation - from the Light of the world. This was the greatest "WOW" moment ever.

I felt inspired, uplifted, excited. I wanted to tell everybody about my epiphany, but was afraid they would laugh me right out of Alaska. But I couldn't shake this radical thought that had just exploded in me - and now the answer to why God made all these trees was staring me right in the face: *Trees Represented the Cross. Christ died on a tree. I got it.* I felt at that moment that this was the literally the biggest hint that God could have possibly dropped on the world.

When I got back from our trip, I started doing research immediately on some of the Earth's biggest living creatures. Here's what I discovered:

The largest mammal is the blue whale and the tallest mammal is the giraffe. Blue whales can reach a length of 100 ft. and giraffes a height of 18 feet.

But what ARE the largest living things? They *are* TREES! Trees can stretch up to an astounding 360 feet, dwarfing every other living creature in comparison.

Trees are also some of the Earth's oldest creations! The oldest Sequoia trees are around 3,500 years old. What's more, there are even some olive trees in Jerusalem that were around when Jesus was alive, and I saw them! I was fortunate enough to have visited Israel in 2018. I understand also that there are some select trees dating back 4,000 to 5,000 years. Holy mackerel! Trees are designed to last.

But they last because of their strong, deep roots. How's that for ingenious design? The deeper the roots go, the stronger the tree gets. Also, with strong roots, the better the tree can nourish itself and withstand the nasty weather that comes along.

Then - I couldn't wait to crack open a concordance to see a long list of Bible verses referencing TREES. Well, I did and there were over 100 verses about them.

Huh? I was both shocked and let down. I hardly found anything about a tree directly relating to the cross. I was puzzled.

But then it finally occurred to me: if indeed scripture actually revealed to humanity that trees were a hint from God - and that Christ died on a cross made from one of them - then it would be blatantly *obvious* to all of us. Our salvation wouldn't be by faith alone, but by *sight*. What's more, this would make His Word so *easy* to believe. What kind of faith is that to God? Is it faith at all?

That is the kind of faith where we believe just because we have heard and seen, not wonder whether there's something more lurking beneath the surface. No, Paul said:

> "For we walk by faith and not by sight."
>
> 2 Corinthians 5:7

The author of Hebrews also says to believe by faith. So many times, this encompasses the unseen.

> "Now faith is confidence in what we hope for and assurance about what we do not see."
>
> Hebrews 11:1

But, in this case, is it really unseen? We can't help but see Him in nature:

> "For since the creation of the world God's invisible qualities—his eternal power and divine nature— have been clearly seen, being understood from what has been made, so that people are without excuse."
>
> Romans 1:20

God made trees HUGE. We have no excuse! There is no disguise here. God *wants* us to see trees. I even joked to my husband one day driving down the freeway. I said "God designed the best and biggest billboard system in the world -TREES!" Not only are trees living symbols of His saving grace, but they're gorgeous - just like they were on our train ride in Alaska.

Aren't trees everywhere? Just think of where you're sitting reading this book right now. If there was no basement, floor, cement, carpet, car or street underneath you, what would be there? Probably a tree.

CHAPTER 5

TREE CHATTER

"One generation commends your works to another;
they tell of your mighty acts.
They speak of the glorious splendor of your majesty—
and I will meditate on your wonderful works."
Psalm 145:4-5

When I got back home to Brunswick, I could hardly wait to tell all my Christian friends about my incredible epiphany. My good friend Julie and I went for a walk, as we often do, ironically through the beautiful Cleveland Metroparks System with thousands of trees all around us. Surprisingly, that walk helped develop my theory even further.

During that walk, we were both blown away by the notion that the wood from trees could very well be the chosen material on which Christ saved the world.

It was like playing verbal ping-pong; Julie and I just kept

bouncing ideas off of each other over and over and over again. We thought of so many examples of how wood saved people in the scriptures. Of course, the most important one: the CROSS. But there were so many other roles that the wood of trees played for saving people in biblical history.

- **Noah's Ark** - Genesis 6:14
- **The Burning Bush** - Exodus 3:2
- **Moses' Staff** - Exodus 4:17
- **Sacrificial Wood** - Genesis 6:14
- **The Ark of the Covenant** - Exodus and Deuteronomy
- **David's Palace** - 2 Samuel 5:11
- **Solomon's Palace and Temple** - 1 Kings 5; 6:1,38

We blurted out each thought of other tree related biblical facts:

- **Adam and Eve - tree leaves covered their nakedness** - Genesis 3: 7
- **Jesus and His Father were Both Carpenters** - Matthew 13:55
- **The Garden of Eden - housed magnificent trees, all giving great pleasure** - Genesis 2:9
- **The Tree of "Good and Evil"** - Genesis 2:9
- **The Tree of Life** - Proverbs 11:30; Proverbs 13:12; Proverbs15:4; Genesis2:9; Genesis3:22; Revelation2:7; Revelation 22:2
- **Fruit of the Spirit** - from trees - Galatians 5:22-23

- **Branches of Palm Trees** - the followers of Jesus took and went out to meet him as He travelled into Jerusalem - John 12:13 🌴
- **The Passover Doorpost with blood from the lamb** - Exodus 12:7 🚪
- **Jesus said "I am the vine and you are the branches"** - John 15:5 🍃
- The **Crown of Thorns** - Matthew 27:29 👑

We both froze as she stated this stunning thought:

- **THE BIBLE ITSELF IS MADE FROM PAPER!!**

And then, Julie stopped dead in her tracks and noted yet another amazing fact:

- **THE MANGER WAS MADE FROM WOOD**

We both gasped as we reviewed our list. But the basics were incredible. The manger was made of wood and held Christ as a babe. Later, the cross was made of wood and held Christ as He died for us. Both woods saved, protected and gave us new life. Amazing!

Now in our lives, Julie and I blurted out our own tree uses:

- Trees give life - giving oxygen we need to breathe O
- Trees provide wood for fires for warmth 🔥
- Trees were cut for wood stoves for cooking 🍳
- Trees provide safe environments to house the animals in the circle of life - crucial to our own existence 🦓

In essence, trees are the purest essential God gives us for life. Now *and* later.

Julie and I couldn't stop chattering about trees. We couldn't believe how many wood references that were coming to mind. Paper that renders stories; benches that comfort wonderers; bookcases that hold wisdom; trees that provide shade and nests for birds and critters; beautiful backdrops in yards and parks; comfort, joy, peace.

There were so many essential uses for wood, but I kept coming back to the cross. I couldn't shake the new and astounding thought that God's greatest hint to humanity might be through trees, representing the means to eternal life. It was all because of Christ's act of humility.

> "God, did not consider equality with God something to be used to his own advantage; rather, he made himself nothing by taking the very nature[b] of a servant, being made in human likeness. And being found in appearance as a man, he humbled himself by becoming obedient to death—even death on a cross!"
>
> Philippians 2: 5b-8

After my amazing walk with Julie, I began looking at city and neighborhood sites around me.

- Trees provide wood used to build houses and structures to protect us ▩

- Trees build churches to worship

- Trees make Telephone poles for communication †

- Trees make bridges to cross over

- Trees have made vehicles and sea-going vessels on which to travel

- Trees make the walls in buildings where we work

- Trees make tables for gathering for fellowship and food

- Trees are what make the furniture where we sit and sleep

- Trees are what make most doors. We have to pass through them daily to enter and exit the comfort and protection of our homes

Structures mentioned above were mostly all built with horizontal and vertical foundations - with cross shaped beams. Crosses create strength and support! Ah-ha, all possibly more hints from God regarding *crosses on the inside.* More information about that will be in the next chapter. But in the meantime…

…is all this man-made construction from trees a plea from God to the ones making them?

CHAPTER 6

CROSSES...ALL AROUND AND INSIDE US

"For the message of the cross is foolishness to those
who are perishing, but to us who are being saved
it is the power of God."
I Corinthians 1:18

Crosses are made from trees, yes, but we don't just see crosses at the top of churches or others made from wood. Crosses are all around us - and even *inside* us.

Check out these locations, starting with this interesting one:

+ If you're able to, get up from where you are sitting and go look at the inside of your front door. Are you there? Most of you will see six panels. Now look between the panels, you will see perfect crosses! In the 1700's, a six panel door was an expression of Christian faith (This is yet another brainstorm from my dear friend Julie!)

+ In our bodies there is a protein network called Laminin, a foundation for most of our cells and organs. It is in the shape of a cross (Google it!)

+ While you're surfing Google, check out the image of a skeleton. Now look at the rib section. Ribs were formed in the shape of strong crosses to protect our most vital organs - especially our life sustaining heart

+ Crosses are logos for charities like the Red Cross and companies of health services like BlueCross/BlueShield

+ Crosses are on hospital and emergency room signs

+ Crosses are the logos of companies that make medical uniforms for companies that sell them like White Cross Scrubs

+ A giant red cross is the mark of the US Navy hospital ship that is appropriately named the "Comfort"

+ Crosses are worn around the necks of men and women as a sign of belief

+ Crosses are grafted onto earrings, bracelets, rings, money clips, ties and even belt buckles

+ Crosses are adorned on the walls of homes, nursing homes and churches

+ The "sign of the cross" is made in the Catholic traditions when they start and end their prayers. Also after they receive sacraments

+ Crosses are clutched inside the palms of hurting people for hope
+ Crosses are placed at the site of accidents where families and friends have lost their loved ones
+ Crosses are placed in caskets of the deceased
+ Crosses are signs of memorials everywhere. They are seen throughout cemeteries and especially on the graves of soldiers. Like Christ they served and they protected us
+ We make crosses out of palm leaves at Easter
+ A perfect cross is made when you connect the lines of north, south, east and west on a map
+ Crosses are the shapes of intersections on the road. We pass them for miles when we travel without even noticing
+ Crosses are on the shields of Knights
+ Crosses are built tall, to stand out, and to be seen by thousands of passersby on the side of highways

Now for a little fun "cross" trivia:

+ Isn't it interesting that for our whole lives we've been "crossing" our arms and our legs - right in front of us?

Are these constant reminders? Here's more:

+ When building a fire, we start with two logs laid *crisscrossed*
+ Why do we say "*Cross* my heart"?

+ Cross stich projects make beautiful art. Thread is intertwined on a canvas in the form of *crosses*

Where else do YOU see crosses?

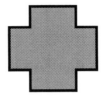

CHAPTER 7

GOD'S FOUR SEASONS OF LOVE

"...for love comes from God."
I John 4:7

During that same fall season of Titus 2 Women's Bible Study, I had the privilege of sharing my theory - albeit timidly–with one of our special guest speakers.

As usual, it was cautiously that I explained my thoughts to her. I was always hesitant that someone would say that my imagination was simply running wild.

I was delighted when the guest immediately lit up. Not only had my theory peaked her curiosity, but now *her own* wheels were turning.

What she said blew me away: "Think of deciduous trees Annette. They are an allegory for our journey of sanctification!"

For those of you who need it, (like I did at the time), here is the definition of *"deciduous"* from Merriam-Webster Dictionary:

> "falling off or shed seasonally or at a certain stage
> of development in the life cycle."

She said, "Think about it. A deciduous tree starts out as a tiny seed, much like we do ourselves in the womb. Also like us, trees go through a long maturation process. Trees are then nourished and drawn out and *changed* by the light."

She was right. We see this maturation process in the deciduous trees all around us - every year especially in the Midwest where I live.

THE FALL

It all starts in the fall, when trees stop photosynthesizing. This causes the leaves to turn brilliant shades of red, orange, yellow, and purple before falling to the ground. In this way, leaves change their old natures to die.

Allegorically, humans begin to shed their old natures when they repent. Like trees, we don't die by any means; we simply accept that we are *changing* as a result of shedding our old habits and accepting God's forgiveness.

"For we know that our old self was crucified with him so that the body of sin might be done away with that we should no long be slave to sin."

Romans 6:6-7

The fall of man is represented by this season - but beautifully resolved by the shedding of sins.

THE WINTER

By winter, trees no longer have any detectable traces of their old nature, or last year's leaves. Oftentimes at the end of winter, trees are pruned to encourage better growth. They stand bare in surrender, waiting for the hope of something better - the hope of new life!

As new Christians, this season of spirituality can be a little scary. We feel completely vulnerable to the unknown. But the Word encourages us to stand strong for abundant life to come.

"I came that they might have life and have it to the full."

John 10:10

THE SPRING

Brand new life begins! The unique placement of the sun prompts plants everywhere to start photosynthesizing again. The light coaxes new leaves out of their little buds, with beautifully-colored and fragrant flowers in tow. Not only is this newfound growth nice to look at, but aromatic as well, sometimes from miles away! Like trees, born-again souls bloom into new life and become fragrant to the Lord and others as well.

> "Therefore, if anyone is in Christ, he is a new creation; the old has gone, the new has come!"
>
> 2 Corinthians 5:17

THE SUMMER

Keep in mind, the pretty blooms of spring don't last for very long. Trees still have meaningful work to do. Eventually, the flowers give way to summer's deep green leaves. Some trees yield sumptuous, nourishing and plentiful fruit to enjoy.

Mature trees provide us with lumber for building and firewood for warmth. Their wood offers us protection, comfort and safety. Trees also make perfect homes for animals - they provide restful atmospheres and beautiful backdrops for yards and parks. One of the most important facts about trees is that they create oxygen for us - *to stay alive!*

It seems that whatever mature summer trees do, mature humans do too. We also bear fruit, nourish others, protect and provide shelter. We make the world a beautiful place by providing backdrops for homes and families and we exhale the air of teaching and encouragement.

> "For we are God's workmanship, created in Christ
> Jesus to do good works, which God prepared in
> advance for us to do."
>
> Ephesians 2:10

We plant seeds where the Holy Spirit's wind blows and reproduce our faith by obeying Christ's great commission:

> "Therefore go and make disciples of all nations,
> baptizing them in the name of the Father and of the
> Son and of the Holy Spirit, and teaching them to
> obey everything I have commanded you. And surely
> I am with you always, to the very end of the age."
>
> Matthew 28:19-20

Summary of the Seasons of a Christian's life:

- <u>Autumn:</u> The fall of man - the shedding of sin
- <u>Winter:</u> The stark and emptiness of surrender
- <u>Spring</u>: Here comes the sun, (the Son!) sprouting new life
- <u>Summer:</u> The glorious fruit of purpose

We Christians can easily interpret the four seasons as how God intends for us to live out our spiritual lives.

Is God trying to speak to us through seasons and how the deciduous trees change? Perhaps He is trying to convey the message to look at the wood that is a part of our salvation! The seasons are so obvious, maybe they are a hint to look at what we must do from the beginning to the end of our spiritual lives.

I can almost hear God chuckling to Himself as He was creating the Earth, thinking that this hint was too obvious. But then again, would people even see the obvious?! After all, the Lord asks us in Mark 8:18, "Do you have eyes, but fail to see?" It really makes you wonder.

Not just deciduous trees but all trees around us seem to teach us to ROOT ourselves in *spiritual* nourishment so that we can defy the gravity of enemy forces and get to work!

> "...And I pray that you, being rooted and established in love, may have power, together with all the saints, to grasp how wide and long and high and deep is the love of Christ and to know this love that surpasses knowledge - that you may be filled to the measure of all the fullness of God."
>
> Ephesians 3:17-19

Deciduous Trees - are they the story of *your* spiritual life?

CHAPTER 8

MAYBE - WELL, PROBABLY

"In the beginning God created the heavens and the earth."

Genesis 1:1

"Once upon a time…"

Did I grab your attention? Don't you just love a good story? We've loved them since childhood! We love them in novels, TV and movies. We love them read from Mom, Grandma, our teachers and our babysitters!

God designed us to love stories. Why? Because I believe He wants us to hear and see His own *epic* story. Stories have been planted in us from both what has been made and God's actual words from the Bible. One of my favorite passages in the Old Testament is this:

"He has planted eternity in the human heart."

Ecclesiastes 3:11 (NLT)

(Coincidently "planted" - is so appropriate for this book!)

I do believe that trees all around us are telling a large part of the great epic God laid out for us. But also I believe there's even more to this story called nature and our own instincts. The pages of His book are lying open for us to see and absorb every day.

John Eldridge expresses this concept perfectly in his critically-acclaimed book, *Epic*. Several profound excerpts from Eldredge's book changed my life.

The first one tells us that nature keeps us longing for paradise.

> "After months and months of winter, I long for the return of summer. Sunshine, warmth, color, and the long days of adventure together. The garden blossoms in all its beauty. The meadows soft and green. Vacation. Holiday. Isn't this what we most deeply long for? To leave the winter of the world behind, what Shakespeare called 'the winter of our discontent,' and find ourselves suddenly in the open meadows of summer?"

The second one describes morning and nighttime's signals.

"Sunrise and sunset tell the tale every day, remembering Eden's glory, foretelling Eden's return."

The third one is in my favorite. Eldredge proclaims this:

"...the earth has all the marks of an artist's hand."

I am in awe of God's story. It's told in everything that we see, even when we look up in the sky. That story was even put to music in the Psalms!

For the director of music. A psalm of David.
"The heavens declare the glory of God;
the skies proclaim the work of his hands.
Day after day they pour forth speech;
night after night they reveal knowledge.
They have no speech, they use no words;
no sound is heard from them.
Yet their voice goes out into all the earth,
their words to the ends of the world.
In the heavens God has pitched a tent for the sun.
It is like a bridegroom coming out of his chamber,
like a champion rejoicing to run his course.
It rises at one end of the heavens

and makes its circuit to the other;

nothing is deprived of its warmth."

Psalm 19:1-6

Please remember, the Bible, the Scriptures, are your literary story from God. But the verse below tells us that *what is made* means that God is defining himself in nature too.

"For since the creation of the world God's invisible qualities - his eternal power and divine nature - have been clearly seen, being understood from what has been made, so that men are without excuse."

Romans 1:20

So, maybe...

- Maybe that's why the sun rises and sets each day to remind us of the dark that came through Adam and Eve's sin, then later, the return of the light - the restoration of paradise
- Maybe that's why people love to get out into the warmth of the sun; it allows them to *feel* the comfort of the Lord
- Maybe that's why people love to "get out" in nature. Maybe God is calling them through it. He could be begging, *"Look at Me!"*
- Maybe that's why people love to take walks or drives through the parks to see the beauty of all the foliage.

Because it's a reminder from the heavens of *how to worship* by lifting glory upward.

- Maybe that's why people love boats and cruises to enjoy vast seas and oceans. The miles of water might be a huge clue to consider the *spiritual cleansing of baptism*

- Maybe that's why people are mesmerized by fire. They are obsessed with the flames that might just point them to *consequences* of sin

- Maybe that's why people leave their homes and instinctively go out to the marketplace to *buy* things. We can understand *value* - and God's *valuing* of us. Remember that He purchased us. "You are bought with a price..." 1 Corinthians 7:23

Maybe - well, probably... But we'll save all of that (and more) for a future book.

What can you discover today in nature, or in your instinct, that is maybe - well, probably, an important message from God?

CHAPTER 9

HOW CHRIST IS EVERGREEN AT CHRISTMAS

"Jesus Christ is the same yesterday
and today and forever."
Hebrews 13:8

Of course, I can't write this book without mentioning Christmas trees.

Christmas trees are Pine trees, and Pine trees are *evergreen.* You could probably guess the meaning based on that word alone; it denotes a tree that never loses its leaves, but stays green forever.

In Alaska, the trees that I saw the most were evergreen trees. What baffled me the most was that these pine trees seemed to completely defy the patterns that God set for all the other trees. They have needles instead of leaves, they don't bear fruit or flowers and they never change color like deciduous trees do.

But then it dawned on me that Hebrews 13:8 says, "Jesus Christ is the same yesterday, today and forever." Perhaps these *never changing* trees represent Christ. So of course we would use, I believe instinctively, pine trees to celebrate Christmas and the birth of Christ.

Think about it. In the winter, the bleakest and stillest of seasons, evergreen trees stand out in the fields and yards. Their rich green color blazes warmly against the barren trees. If this tree represents the *never changing* Christ, I believe it's symbolic, that Christ is all that is left after we've surrendered everything. Winter seems to be *very still* for a reason: so that we can see Christ stand out clearly amid a backdrop of emptiness and dormancy.

Through the bareness of the cold and in many places, snowy season, I hardly believe it's a coincidence that the beauty of evergreen trees is most distinct in the winter. They represent God - the eternal, loving, forgiving, never changing, unbending, and life-giving force that sustains us all. They are beautiful. He is beautiful.

Back to the train ride now in Alaska…I had one more mind-blowing revelation during the miles and miles of trees I saw. It's as if God blessed me with one more sweet answer to my prayer that I asked Him to teach me something new about Himself in Alaska.

As I randomly gazed at the tops of the evergreen trees,

I was once again startled at what I saw. Could this be? Every evergreen tree had an arrow at the top pointing directly to the heavens. It was as if they were begging humanity to look up to acknowledge Christ as Lord. Yet another WOW moment.

Is it possible that people, even non-Christians, are simply expressing what they intuitively know when they choose an evergreen tree at Christmas? I am pretty sure that God wants us to see Him in evergreen trees.

Is it also instinctive to decorate Christmas trees? After all, Christ is to be celebrated! What's the biggest staple of decorating a Christmas tree? Lights! Do we choose to decorate with lights because in our hearts we know it represents our *Light* of the world, just as John 1 says?

> "In him was life, and that life was the light of all
> mankind. The light shines in the darkness, and
> the darkness has not overcome it."
>
> John 1:4-5

Christ *wants* to be celebrated - in royal décor! So then we, as His children, decorate our Christmas trees in glittery ornaments, jewels, beads and all the rest.

Have you noticed how national, state, and city trees are lit and then celebrated in public ceremonies during the Christmas season? They draw people together to enjoy choirs and fireworks for the occasion. Everyone knows that Christmas tree lighting ceremonies are a big deal.

Naturally, I decided to research further the traditions of Christmas tree decorating. I was not surprised in the least to learn that the two most common Christmas tree toppers are stars and angels. Acclaimed Victorian poet Christina Rossetti once wrote:

> "Love came down at Christmas, Love all lovely,
> Love Divine; Love was born at Christmas, Stars
> and Angels gave the sign."

Is it a natural instinct to purchase these two Christmas tree toppers, both of which heralded the birth of Christ? Christmas is a time to commemorate God's greatest gift of love to the world through the birth of a Savior. Angels and stars pointed to this gift in Bethlehem, and they still do to this day! Even unbelievers top their trees with these two symbols. Read Ecclesiastes 3:11 again.

We also set our gifts to each other under our trees to beautify the scene. These gifts could indeed represent the myriad of gifts that Christ has given to each of us. Talents, love, truth, pleasures, shelter, food. The list goes on and on.

> "Each of you should use whatever gift you have received to serve others, as faithful stewards of God's grace in its various forms".
>
> I Peter 4:10

Have you heard of a Chrismon Tree? A Chrismon tree is one that is decorated with the ornaments representing the attributes of Christ. At my church, we decorate our main tree in the style of a Chrismon tree. A plethora of felt figures, sewn by church members are used. I didn't think decorating a tree could get any more appropriate! Here we were, Christ's bride, celebrating new life, coming together to decorate the tree with objects that represent His majesty!

One Sunday morning during service, I kept staring at the Chrismon tree in the sanctuary. I was surprised to see neither a traditional star nor angel atop the tree. Instead, we place a golden crown on the top bough. Does this crown not designate exactly who Christ is? Maybe the angel or star didn't need to show us this time. We knew it. Our worship was based on it. He is our King!

Endearingly, Christmas trees are the center of family and friend celebrations. Christopher Radko, author of *The Heart of Christmas*, writes:

> "...the central Icon of the season is the Christmas tree. I can't imagine the holidays without the magic of wonderfully decorated trees, each different, each special. Like the hearth or a dining table, a Christmas tree draws people to it - and to one another."

From this, we can see that the Christmas tree is not only the symbol of this divine love and new life; but it unites people in forgiving love, if only for the briefest of moments. Most everyone loves the holidays because it's a time of joy spent with family and friends.

Radko goes on to explore what specifically it is about evergreen trees that compels us to associate them with Christmas:

> "Our visceral response to evergreens makes me wonder if they have magical properties we have long forgotten. The scents of pine, spruce, and fir trees not only connect us to the natural world, [but] they actually cheer and invigorate us. No wonder aroma therapists use the essential oils of evergreens for their energizing and healing properties."

There is something naturally energizing about evergreen trees, even in their scent. It's as if every single property of evergreen trees is designed to invigorate us and persuade us to celebrate hope and new life!

After the exchange I had with my guest speaker that day at Titus 2 class, she emailed me a verse from Isaiah that hinted strongly at God's message about trees:

> "Instead of the thorn bush will grow the juniper, and instead of briers the myrtle will grow. This will be for the Lord's renown, for an everlasting sign, that will endure forever."
>
> Isaiah 55:13

The original Hebrew uses the word *"beros"* for a pine tree, which directly translates to cypress or fir. In *Observing God's World* by Gregory Rickard and Gregory Parker, we learn that firs are popular for lumber and papermaking, and are attractive as Christmas trees for their fragrant smell. Pine oil is now sold as a comforting aroma.

> "But thanks be to God, who always leads us as captives in Christ's triumphal procession and uses us to spread the aroma of the knowledge of him everywhere."
>
> 2 Corinthians 2:14

If you couldn't already tell, I've taken a real liking to evergreen trees since my life-changing trip to Alaska.

How much of eternity is written on the hearts of those who buy Christmas trees? *(Remember Ecclesiastes 3:11!)*

CHAPTER 10

LIKE CEDARS OF LEBANON

*"... I myself will take a shoot from the very top of a cedar
and plant it; I will break off a tender sprig from its topmost
shoots and plant it on a high and lofty mountain. ... it will
produce branches and bear fruit and become a splendid cedar.
Birds of every kind will nest in it; they will find shelter
in the shade of its branches."*
Ezekiel 17:22-23

What a beautiful tree! You've likely heard of it - a Cedar of
Lebanon. Yet another evergreen!

The country of Lebanon proudly displays this popular tree
in the center of its national flag.

The Hebrew word for cedar is *"erez"* and it is mentioned
in the Bible over 70 times! It was used for wood in the Old

Testament because of its high quality. It was easy to work with and easily shaped.

Aside from having many of the never changing attributes of Christ, like the evergreens mentioned in Chapter 9, it also models what the Christian life should be like.

God says that we should grow tall like the Cedars of Lebanon (Psalm 92:12). They are stately, always green, slow-growing, long branched, so enduring, and sweet-smelling.

Smith's Bible Dictionary, written over a hundred years ago, mentions that one of these trees living on Mount Lebanon was 70 feet tall, 63 feet in circumference, and was believed to be 2,000 years old!

One writer said that the roots of these cedars could go as far down into the ground as the tree was tall—they have foundations that are not easily destroyed. Hosea speaks of its roots:

> "I will be like the dew to Israel;
> he will blossom like a lily.
> Like a cedar of Lebanon
> he will send down his roots;
> his young shoots will grow.
> His splendor will be like an olive tree,
> his fragrance like a cedar of Lebanon."
>
> Hosea 14:5-6

These mammoth cedar trees start as little seedlings that are sometimes pulled up and eaten by hungry grazing animals. If they survive long enough to gain some size, they can then endure storms, drought, and other seasonal environmental challenges. Each year, pushing their roots deeper and deeper into the soil, they build strength by gaining a more solid footing. (Inspired From *Forerunner Commentary*)

Now enjoy this passage in Ezekiel 31 that describes the majestic Cedar of Lebanon:

> *"In the eleventh year, in the third month on the first day, the word of the LORD came to me: 'Son of man, say to Pharaoh King of Egypt and to his hordes:*

Who can be compared with you in majesty?
Consider Assyria, once a cedar in Lebanon,
with beautiful branches overshadowing the forest;
it towered on high,
its top above the thick foliage.
The waters nourished it,
deep springs made it grow tall;
their streams flowed
all around its base
and sent their channels
to all the trees of the field.
So it towered higher
than all the trees of the field;
its boughs increased
and its branches grew long,
spreading because of abundant waters.
All the birds of the sky

nested in its boughs,
all the animals of the wild
gave birth under its branches;
all the great nations
lived in its shade.
It was majestic in beauty,
with its spreading boughs,
for its roots went down
to abundant waters.
The cedars in the garden of God
could not rival it,
nor could the junipers
equal its boughs,
nor could the plane trees
compare with its branches—
no tree in the garden of God
could match its beauty.
I made it beautiful
with abundant branches,
the envy of all the trees of Eden
in the garden of God.'"

Ezekiel 31: 1-9

Cedars are rooted, grounded, fragrant, easily shaped and used. Aren't the qualities of this tree what Christians should aspire to?

CHAPTER 11

OH EASTER TREE, OH EASTER TREE!

"The God of our Fathers raised Jesus from the dead -
whom you had killed by hanging him on a tree."
Acts 5:30

Oh Easter Tree, Oh Easter Tree… Oops, wrong song!

But wait - one dear friend of mine just recently pointed out to me that some pine trees actually grow *crosses* in the spring around Easter! What?!

Sure enough, I looked it up and found a picture. (See above. It's true!) What grows is a spectacular display of crosses sprouting upward! The color…GOLD!

> "Ever seen a cross on top of a pine tree? No, not
> the wooden kind. Around Easter each spring,

some species in certain regions start to develop shoots with a familiar shape. This sighting has led to a popular legend that pine trees "know" when it's Easter.

If you look at the tops of the pine trees two weeks before [Easter], you will see the yellow shoots. As the days get closer to Easter Sunday, the tallest shoot will branch off and form a cross. By the time Easter Sunday comes around, you will see that most of the pine trees will have small yellow crosses on all of the tallest shoots."

Country Living Magazine-
Taysha Murtaugh, March 28, 2018

Could this evergreen tree that commemorates the brutal death of our Savior with the growth of golden crosses, be yet another tree to be surrounded with joyful songs once a year?

You might ask though, "How could anyone sing with *joy* - about *death*?"

If Christ could have joy about His own death, we can have joy about His death too. Read the following passage. You will probably be astounded, like I was, at these eight simple words: "*for the joy that was set before him*". How could a person possibly experience joy during beating, bruising, being spit on, being nailed to a cross and mocked?

"Looking to Jesus, the founder and perfecter of our faith, who *for the joy that was set before him*

endured the cross, despising the shame, and is
seated at the right hand of the throne of God."

Hebrews 12:2 w/Emphasis

During the Easter season, especially on Good Friday, will the
wood of the trees in your neighborhood be a stark reminder of
that day long ago when Jesus gave His life, like those with the
golden crosses at the top?

CHAPTER 12

LOOKING FOR GOD ALL AROUND US

"Let everything that has breath
praise the LORD! Hallelujah!"
Psalm 150:6

That spring, before we went on our cruise, I prayed that God would teach me something new and delightful about Himself in Alaska. I repeated this prayer over and over on my intimate walks with Him.

Is it pure coincidence or is it really God who answered my prayers by bringing these tree theories to the forefront of my mind? Had He really taught me something new about Himself just as I had asked? Even as these are only theories, I still feel compelled to share them with others, both in speaking engagements and in this book.

It seems that simply sharing about trees becomes a form of evangelism. Even if I can't convert some with my theories, I can at least help people to look at trees in a new and wholly unexpected way. Who knows, maybe I can even convince an atheist or agnostic to make a connection with the cross. One can only hope!

I have to admit that I'm still not sure if God answered my pre-cruise prayers by inspiring me with these tree theories. It all seemed to make perfect sense to me. I will, however, know someday in heaven.

> "For now we see only a reflection as in a mirror;
> then we shall see face to face. Now I know in part;
> then I shall know fully, even as I am fully known."
>
> I Corinthians 13:12

The following drives my tree theories and is my own personal WOW verses. You have already read it in this book a few times because I believe it is so profound to this subject:

> "God has made it plain to them. For since the creation of the world, God's invisible qualities, His eternal power and divine nature, have been clearly seen, being understood from what has been made, so that men are without excuse."
>
> Romans 1:19-20

When I searched for the original Greek translation of the word *"made"*, I was happy to see that it translated to *"creation or workmanship.*" This idea of divine creation should not surprise us, as both we and nature are all living examples of God's creative heart!

After you finish and close this book, please take a look around. How much do you see God at work? Here are some reminders of what hints He likely is sending your way:

+ Look at the cross hanging in your church. Remember, it and the real one was made from the wood of trees
+ Look at the pages of your Bible. Remember, paper is from trees
+ Look at the buildings that line your city's streets. Remember, the lumber from trees provides shelter, protection, and safety
+ Breathe in a soothing breath of oxygen. Remember, it's coming from a nearby tree

Our hearts naturally long for our Creator. He made us this way.

+ Look at your holiday décor. Remember, a beautifully lit Christmas tree could represent the actual coming of the Light of the world, Jesus Christ. We celebrate, exchange gifts, sing, ring bells, eat delicious food and spend quality time with loved ones around this annual centerpiece.

"My heart says of You, 'Seek His face!'"

Psalm 27:8a

As you decorate your Christmas tree this year, ask yourself these questions:

- Why do I want to decorate it?
- Why do the lights wrap all the way around?
- Why do I so long to celebrate what it represents?
- Why do I sing songs about it?
- Why is the word "BELIEVE" on tree ornaments?
- Why an angel or star at the top?

If your answers are uncertain, simply review this verse once again:

"He has also placed eternity in the hearts of men."

Ecclesiastes 3:11

Are non-believers blind to God's HINT through trees at Christmas, or for that matter, are they blind to all the trillions of huge trees that are all around them throughout the year?

CHAPTER 13

"YOU'LL SEE, ANTHONY!!"

*"Our mouths were filled with laughter, our tongues
with songs of joy. Then it was said among the nations,
'The Lord has done great things for them.'"*
Psalms 126:2

I'd like to share one last story.

The night after I returned home from Alaska, I had praise
team rehearsal at church. When it was done, I was pooped and
I plopped down onto one of the front seats. The praise team's
young drummer, Anthony, came and sat down next to me.

"How ya doin' Annette?" he said. "What's new?" I lit up.
And suddenly, with renewed energy, I yelped, "Thanks for
asking Anthony!", then began to gush about my train ride to
the Klondike and my *new* tree theory!

Well, it happened! Ugh. One of the first people I told teased me about it.

Anthony said, "Annette, that sounds like a pretty cool vacation you took, but I think your theory about trees being a giant hint from God, is just a little *far-fetched*."

With all my enthusiasm still reeling, this is how I answered, "Anthony, someday when we get to heaven, we'll be sitting next to each other on a bench made from a tree, under the shade of a tree, with birds singing in the tree. And at that moment, I pray that the Lord will walk right up to you with a big grin on His face, put His finger on your nose just to let you know:

Palmer got it!"

Thank you for taking the time to explore my newfound theory about trees being God's hint to humanity. As I explained in the beginning of this book, my yearly Titus 2 Women's Bible study has been teaching all about connecting with others. But the connection I so encourage you to cultivate today is the most important one. It is an eternal connection with the God of the universe. His HINTS are all around you. He longs for you to notice.

So now, go forth and GROW. Get acquainted just a bit more, with the glorious Artist and Creator of - TREES!

EPILOGUE

To the believers reading this book, I pray you were enlightened!

For those of you who have not had a connection with God *yet*, I hope you will start to see a message from the trees all around you. Have you equated them to the material that was used for the cross of Jesus Christ? If so, you might want to consider, right now, connecting for the first time with their Creator.

Here's how you do it. Know first, how God sees you according to the bible:

1. **You (and the rest of us) have missed the mark:**

   "For all have sinned and fall short of the glory of God."
   Romans 3:23

2. **God loves you and has a wonderful plan for your life:**

   "I have come that they may have life, and have it to the full."

   John 10:10

3. **God has created a bridge for you to heaven - the Cross.**

"For God so loved the world that he gave his one and only Son, that whoever believes in him shall not perish but have eternal life."

John 3:16

Then simply pray this prayer to start your eternal connection:

"Lord, I know I have missed your mark and I am sorry for it. Thank you for being willing to forgive me for my sins and open up the heavens to me when I die.

Now, please make me the kind of person you'd like me to be"

If you prayed that prayer, and are willing to make Jesus Christ the Lord of your life, then you can now celebrate salvation. The following verse makes it clear:

"I write these things to you who believe in the name of the Son of God so that you may <u>know</u> that you have eternal life."

John 5:13 (Emphasis added)

The above prayer is how I started my conversion. I can only tell you this: to know and connect with your God, personally and intimately, will be the best decision of your life. It is by far, the purest, most reliable and faithful relationship of all.

If you connected, YOU are now a NEW CREATION.

"Therefore, if anyone is in Christ, the new creation
has come: The old has gone, the new is here!"
2 Corinthians 5:17

Please tell a trusted believer if you prayed that prayer today. The telling will strengthen you.

Feel free to contact me or visit my website for more encouragement to grow.

God bless your new growth!

Feel free to contact me or visit my website for more encouragement to grow at

www.TreesGodsHintBook.com

Annette Palmer is an author and speaker from Brunswick, Ohio. As a voice major at the University of Southern California, she became a full time private music teacher, with emphasis in singing and piano. She's a wife, married to Bob, a Mom to Curtis, a Toastmaster, Sunday school teacher and church musician. She is blessed with wonderful family and friends.

If there wasn't a floor where you're sitting or standing, what would be there? Probably a tree.

Have you looked around lately? TREES are everywhere! Why?

Are trees possibly a hint from God to humanity? Annette Palmer explains why she believes they are.

Explore the landscape from a train's window. Reminisce about your past Christmases, your last walk in the woods, your last drive down the freeway. Fill your thoughts with how amazing nature is. Connect with God like never before through the largest living creatures on Earth, TREES!

> *"If God were a poet, He'd probably say, 'Every time you see a TREE, it's a HINT TO HUMANITY!'"*
>
> *Bob Palmer* (Annette's husband)

Printed in the United States
By Bookmasters